Black's Picture Sports

SMALL BOAT SAILING

Black's Picture Sports

SMALL BOAT SAILING

Norman Dahl

Adam and Charles Black · London

First published 1979 by
A & C Black (Publishers) Ltd
35 Bedford Row, London WC1R 4JH

ISBN 0 7136 1915 5
© Norman Dahl 1979

Dahl, Norman
Small boat sailing. – (Black's picture sports).
1. Sailing
I. Title
797.1′24   GV811.6

ISBN 0-7136-1915-5

Cover by Alistair Black

Line drawings by Colin Paine

Photos:
1 P Davies; 2 and back cover RYA National
Hornet Class Association; 3 IDTV Enterprises
Ltd; 4 Tim Hore, Fireball International;
5 Terry Cherrill, Mirror Class Association;
6 Enterprise Association

The author would like to acknowledge
the help of the RYA Seamanship
Foundation for Figure 20

Set and Printed in Great Britain by
Page Bros (Norwich) Ltd,
Mile Cross Lane, Norwich

Contents

1 Introduction

Small boat sailing is more than a sport; it is a pastime which can be enjoyed in many ways, at any age and at any level of skill. For those who like competition, it offers the possibility of close and exciting racing in a wide variety of dinghy classes at many levels. To race a dinghy really well calls for the same combination of talent, skill, training and fitness that is needed in any sport; but at club level, the beginner is always welcome. He (or she) will almost certainly finish last in his first few races, but it will not be long before he starts to work his way through the fleet towards the front. And there is no doubt that racing is the finest and quickest way to learn how to handle a small boat under sail.

However, small boat sailing does not have to be competitive, and many people go sailing to get away from the competition and stress of daily life. Sailing is a wonderful way of relaxing. Some people like to potter around in enclosed waters, while others make adventurous cruises in the open sea. I know of one intrepid soul and his wife who have even cruised a dinghy from England to Iceland! The bigger boats may be used for camping, and can be made very snug, moored to the bank with a tent cover over the boom, and a kettle quietly hissing over a stove. As with racing, you can find a level of cruising to suit your own inclinations.

Another aspect of small boat sailing is that it is not the exclusive preserve of the young, fit, highly trained athlete. You can sail and race at any age, and in club competition it is often possible for a crafty older helmsman to sail rings round his younger and more impetuous rivals. At the top levels of racing, it is essential to be fit, because all the competitors are at much the same level of skill. The person who sails hardest has the best chance of winning, yet skill and experience are still of vital importance.

Many beginners approach sailing with the firm conviction that it is difficult to learn. In fact, sailing is the straightforward application of simple principles, in order to trap energy from the wind and convert it into the forward motion of the boat. The wind plays only a small part in life on shore, and it is invisible; some of the ways in which a wind behaves are not immediately obvious, and Chapter 3 describes the general principles by which it is possible to harness the wind to make a boat go along.

Another difficulty which faces the newcomer to sailing is the strange and impenetrable language with which sailors surround themselves. No doubt this is often used merely to impress the landlubbers, but it is a good idea for the beginner to learn the proper terms used by seamen. These terms have evolved over many hundreds of years, and describe quickly and accurately what is happening. For example, it is often necessary to refer directions in a boat to the direction from which the wind is blowing, because the progress of the boat is determined by the wind. You could say to a helmsman, 'turn the boat towards the direction from which the wind is blowing'. He would doubtless understand you and do the right thing. But it is easier and quicker to say 'luff', which means exactly the same. Chapter 2 of this book illustrates many of the terms used by seamen to describe their boats and what goes on around them. Other terms are introduced throughout the book, as they are needed, and you will find definitions in the glossary on page 95.

The later chapters of the book are intended to help you get more out of your boat once you have learned how it works – better boat-handling in Chapter 4, more speed in Chapter 5, and more cunning in Chapter 6, which deals with the rules of racing. But this book, like any other book on sailing, is only part of what you need to become a sailor. It is possible to teach yourself from a book and by experimenting on the water, but it is a good idea to get a few lessons, formal or informal, from someone who knows what to do. An experienced friend can probably teach you enough in an afternoon to get you started on a proper basis. From then on, every sailor spends the rest of his life learning more about his boat and how to handle it.

An excellent, if rather more expensive way of learning to sail is to attend one of the many sailing schools now in operation. A typical course will last a week, and most of them lead to one or other of the proficiency awards offered by the Royal Yachting Association. A proficiency award is by no means essential, but it does represent a sound and worthwhile foundation upon which to build your further experience.

Training also helps to ensure that you do not run yourself or your crew into danger without realising it, and gives you an idea of what to do if things start to go wrong.

Good sailing!

The International Laser, designed by Bruce Kirby. Sail numbers now exceed 70,000 world-wide, and the class is growing at the rate of 10,000 a year.

2 The Boat and its Equipment

SAFETY

The water is a potentially dangerous place for the unwise or the unwary. Before you go out in a boat, you should run through the following safety checklist, and if you are taking someone else with you, then you should make sure that he or she is properly prepared as well.

1 You, and anyone else in the boat, should be able to swim, and be able to work in water.

2 You should wear a lifejacket or a buoyancy aid of an approved type. A lifejacket to the full British Standard specification is very efficient at keeping you afloat, but it is rather difficult to work in, so the most practical form of flotation is a buoyancy aid made to the Ship and Boat Builders' National Federation (SBBNF) standard. This gives less buoyancy than a lifejacket, but it is easier to work in. The most comfortable kind are the ones that are put on like a waistcoat.

3 You should protect yourself against cold. Even in high summer it can get very cold indeed on the water, and in spring and autumn, positively arctic. This is not just a matter of personal comfort; cold water can kill, no matter how well you can swim, and you need to protect yourself. Many keen dinghy sailors wear wet suits, which are excellent, if rather expensive.

4 Make sure that the boat is seaworthy, paying particular attention to the buoyancy that the boat carries to keep it afloat in case of accident.

5   Make sure that you know and understand the pro-
    cedure for righting the boat after a capsize, and for
    picking up a man overboard (Chapter 4).

6   Unless you are sailing in close company with others
    (in a race, for example), then make sure that someone
    on shore knows where you are going and when you
    expect to return, so that they can raise the alarm if you
    are overdue. You should also carry some flares or
    orange smoke signals to attract attention if you get
    into difficulties.

RIGGING THE BOAT

Figures 1 and 2 show the parts of a boat and the parts of a
sail. You will rapidly become familiar with these terms as
you sail more. The first time you rig your boat, you will be
faced with the most confusing jumble of spars, ropes and
sails, but it will all quickly fall into place, and you will
soon be able to rig your boat in a matter of minutes.

Each class of boat is rigged differently, but there are
certain aspects in common. The first operation is to step
the mast. In most boats, the mast is supported by three
wires – the forestay, to the bow of the boat, and two
shrouds, one on each side. Either the shrouds or the forestay will be adjustable, so that the mast can be held firmly
in the correct position. However, some boats (the
Optimist, for example) have an unsupported mast, and
some bigger dinghies have more complicated standing
rigging, as these supporting wires are called.

All dinghies have at least one spar, the boom which
supports the foot of the sail. Some boats, like the Mirror
and the Ideal, have another spar, called the gaff, which
carries the head of the mainsail above the top of the mast,
but most dinghies have a Bermudan rig, in which the
mast is made taller and the gaff dispensed with. The
Optimist has an unusual spar called a sprit, which goes
diagonally across the sail.

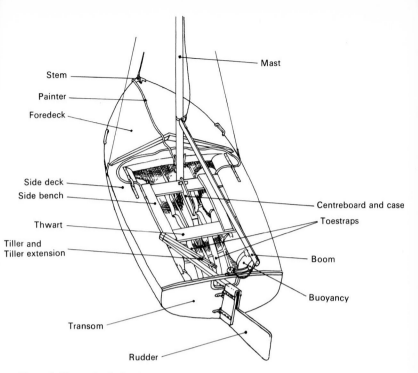

Figure 1. The parts of a boat

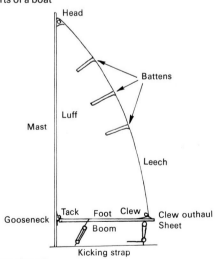

Figure 2. The parts of a sail

13

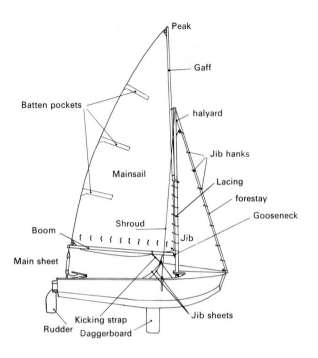

Figure 3. A gunter rigged dinghy. Bermudan rig is similar, but there is no gaff, and the mast is taller

The simplest form of centreboard is called a dagger board, and is merely a flat piece of wood which is pushed down into the plate case, possibly held in position by a piece of shock cord. A more advanced, and in many ways better, way of doing it is to hinge the centreboard on a pivot, and then to control its position with a line. In bigger dinghies with a metal centreboard, a winch is provided to raise the centreboard, which can be quite heavy. In most boats, the rudder blade is also pivoted, so that it can be lifted up in shallow water.

The sails are the motive power of the boat, in the same way that an engine powers a car. They are made of synthetic cloth impregnated with resin to stop the wind blowing through the weave, and most dinghies have two –

a mainsail and a foresail, or jib. Some dinghies may have a third sail, called a spinnaker, made of nylon, which will be discussed further in Chapter 5. The sails are hoisted up the mast by the halyard, and the mainsail is supported at the bottom by a boom. Some boats have a gaff, which supports the upper part of the mainsail, but high performance dinghies all set their mainsails on a tall mast, in Bermudan rig. The luff of the jib is clipped to the forestay by hanks, to keep the luff straight, and the tack is made fast to the stem fitting. The halyard is fixed to the head of the sail, which can then be hoisted. Two sheets are attached to the clew of the sail, one for each side of the boat.

In Bermudan rigged boats, the mainsail is hoisted to the top of the mast, with the luff of the sail running in a groove up the mast. In gunter rigged boats (Mirror, Ideal), the top part of the mainsail luff is fitted into a groove on the gaff, and then the gaff is hoisted on the halyard. In high performance boats, the foot of the mainsail is held by a groove in the boom like the one in the mast, but simpler boats often have a loose-footed mainsail, which is only secured to the boom at the tack and the clew. The mainsail is controlled by the main sheet, which is normally some form of purchase, that is, a pulley, using blocks to obtain a mechanical advantage so that the sail can be controlled easily. This is either attached to the end of the boom and some form of horse on the transom, or else is fixed in the middle of the boom, leading down to a traveller in the centre of the boat.

To rig your boat, then, you should first park it so that it is facing into the wind, and then step the mast. Set up the shrouds and the forestay so that they are tight and hold the mast in the correct position; in simple dinghies, this means getting the mast vertical with respect to the boat, but more complicated boats (best avoided by beginners) have various adjustments to control the rake of the mast and its bend. With the mast properly set up, you can then bend on (attach) the mainsail. The procedure depends upon the rig of the boat. With a

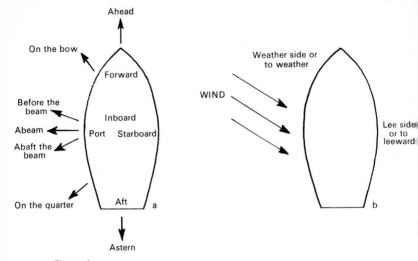

Figure 4.
a Place and direction in a boat
b Direction relative to the wind

Bermudan rig, the head of the sail is attached to the halyard, which runs down from the top of the mast. The sail is then hoisted most of the way, at the same time feeding the rope on the luff (leading edge) of the sail into the groove in the mast. With gaff rig, the top part of the luff is slid into the groove on the gaff and the head of the sail is made fast to the top of the gaff. The gaff is then attached to the halyard and gaff and sail are hoisted together. With the sail almost all the way up, the boom can be fitted to the swivel fitting (gooseneck) on the mast and the clew of the sail (the outer corner) made fast to the end of the boom. If the boom has a groove along its top, then the rope along the foot of the sail must be slid into the groove as the boom is fitted. The tack of the sail is made fast near the gooseneck and the halyard is used to hoist the sail right up, with the luff of the sail taut. The main sheet (which controls the set of the sail) and the kicking strap (which stops the boom rising up) are then attached to the boom, and the mainsail is set.

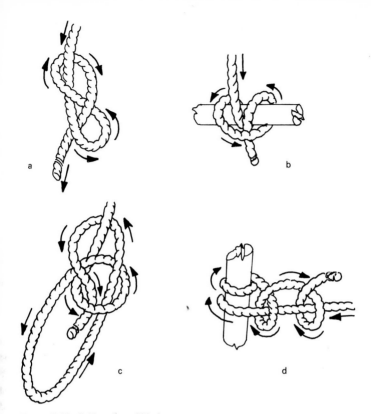

Figure 5. Useful bends and hitches
a Figure 8 knot – a stopper at the end of sheets and halyards
b Clove hitch – for securing to a ring or spar
c Bowline – for making a loop in a rope
d Round turn and two half hitches – a good hitch for securing a boat to a ring or post

Bending on the jib is a much simpler operation; the tack of the sail is made fast to the stem fitting, the plastic hanks along the luff of the sail are clipped around the forestay and the halyard is attached to the head. The sail is then hoisted, and the luff of the sail is made as taut as possible. Two sheets are attached to the clew of the sail, one running to each side. These often take the form of a single piece of rope fixed in the middle, leaving two tails. Rigging the boat is normally done on shore, and the sails are then dropped for launching; however, it is possible, though less convenient, to rig a boat while it is afloat.

HELMSMAN AND CREW

Most sailing dinghies are intended for two people, the helmsman and his crew. They have to work together as a team, and the various jobs must be shared out so as to run the boat efficiently. In general, the helmsman is in command; he steers the boat with the helm or tiller and looks after the mainsheet. The crew looks after the jib sheets and the centreboard. Both must move themselves about in the boat so as to keep it upright on different points of sailing (that is, the various directions a boat can sail in relation to the wind) and different wind strengths. When handling a spinnaker, both helmsman and crew have other jobs, but these are described in Chapter 5.

3 How a Sailing Boat Works

This chapter describes in very simple terms the principles upon which a sailing boat works. It contains a certain amount of aerodynamic theory, which may seem difficult at first; but it is worthwhile studying this theory until you understand it, because you need to appreciate the way in which your source of power works in order to get the best out of it. The actual process of sailing a boat boils down to three tasks, all going on at the same time, each of which influences the others. They are:

1 Steering the boat in the right direction, as the wind allows.
2 Trimming the sails so as to extract the maximum power from the wind.
3 Keeping the boat as near upright as possible.

It is not as difficult as it might seem to do three jobs at once because they are all closely related, and as you gain experience you will find that they become almost instinctive, like riding a bicycle. It is often said that a pilot flies an aeroplane 'by the seat of his pants'. A good helmsman sails his boat, not only by the seat of his pants but also by the feel of the wind on his cheek and the pressure of the tiller and sheet on his fingers. He becomes part of the boat, and no longer has to think about what he need do to keep the boat sailing. But it takes experience to reach that stage, and to begin with we need to study the way in which the wind and water act upon the sails and hull.

The National Hornet, designed by Jack Oolt. A high-performance two-man boat, sailed in over 80 fleets in 30 different countries. It is a National Class in Britain, Poland and the Netherlands.

Let us begin by considering the hull. As far as the underwater shape is concerned, a sailing dinghy is relatively long and thin, and it is pointed at the front (the bow). It is not hard to see why this is so. Such a shape will slip easily through the water, and this is important for any vessel, whether it is propelled by sails, oars or engines. But in the case of a sailing dinghy there is another equally important factor. The hull does not only slip forward easily; it also resists any force which tends to push it sideways. As we shall soon see, the force of the sails generally acts at an angle to the centreline of the boat, so the boat would slip sideways if the shape of the hull did not resist lateral movement. On many points of sailing, the resistance of the hull is still not enough for efficiency, and so a daggerboard or centreboard is fitted to increase the lateral resistance. This board is made of wood or metal, and it can be raised or lowered through a slot in the bottom of the boat (this slot is boxed in to prevent the water pouring into the boat).

The direction in which the boat travels is controlled by a rudder, which is operated by a lever fitted to the top, called a tiller (Figure 6). There are two things to remember about the rudder; firstly, it works because the flow of water past it causes it to push the stern of the boat one way or the other. If the boat is not moving, then the rudder has no effect, and if the boat goes backwards (as it sometimes may), then its effect is reversed. The second point is a rich source of confusion for novice helmsmen; if, in Figure 6, the helmsman moves the tiller to *starboard*, then the rudder causes the boat to turn to *port* (and, as Tweedledee would say, contrariwise). There is no cure for this confusion except practice, and every beginner gets it wrong more times than he cares to think about.

A sail may look like a simple piece of cloth, yet it is in fact a very subtle and efficient device, which has been developed over centuries to produce the greatest possible drive from the wind. Very simply, a sail is tightened or loosened by pulling on the sheet. In Figure 7, we are

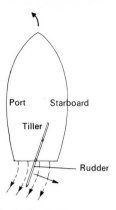

Figure 6. The rudder and tiller. With the boat going forward, moving the tiller to starboard causes the boat to turn to port, and vice versa

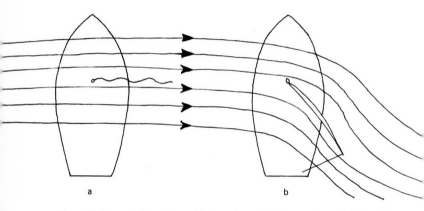

a   b

Figure 7. The wind and the sails. In *a* the sail is free, and merely flaps like a flag. In *b*, the sheet has been hardened in, and the sail is working by altering the flow of wind around it

looking down on a boat with just one sail, the mainsail. The wind is coming over the port beam, and in *a* the sheet controlling the sail is eased, so that the sail merely flaps like a flag. If we pull in on the sheet, the wind will start to fill the sail and it will stop flapping, first at the leech, and then at the luff as well. At this point, the whole sail is still, smoothly curved and full of wind (Figure 7b). Sailors say that the sail has 'gone to sleep',

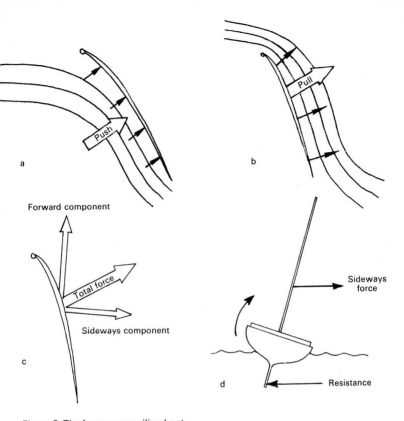

Figure 8. The forces on a sailing boat
a The pressure or push force on the weather side of the sail
b The suction or pull force on the lee side of the sail
c The total of push and pull can be split into two components
d How the sideways force and the resistance of the hull and centreboard make a boat heel

but it is in fact working for you as hard as it can.

Figure 8 shows how the sail produces a force which can be used to push the boat along. There are two components to this force, one of which pushes the boat, and the other pulls it. In Figure 8a, we see that the wind has filled the sail, and it exerts a pressure, just as the wind exerts a pressure on an opened umbrella. The pressure in the sail gives rise to a force which pushes the boat in the direction shown. Figure 8b shows the second component of the force caused by the wind, which is a little more difficult to understand. The curved sail acts rather like an aeroplane wing; by deflecting the airflow and making it travel around the curve of the sail, a suction is generated on the side of the sail away from the wind, and this leads to another force, which pulls the boat along. In many cases this 'pull' force is much bigger than the 'push' force caused by the pressure on the other side of the sail, and it depends upon the smooth flow of air across the sail. If the sail is sheeted in too far, the smooth flow of air is disturbed and the 'pull' force is reduced. If the sail is not sheeted in far enough, then it is not 'asleep', and smooth flow is prevented. The correct sheeting of the sail is vital to good performance, and the sheet should be set so that the sail is just asleep.

In Figure 8c, the 'pull' force and the 'push' force have been combined, leading to a total force on the boat, acting more or less at right angles to the chord of the sail (the line of the boom, if one is fitted). This total force can in turn be broken down into two components. One acts along the centreline of the boat, and actually makes it go forward through the water. The second force, at right angles, tries to push the boat sideways, but the shape of the hull and the centreboard prevent this from happening. Figure 8d shows what happens. The sideways force is exerted from a position about one third of the way up the mast, trying to push the boat sideways. The hull and centreboard resist, producing a force to keep the boat where it is. These two forces tend to make the boat heel, as they act together in what is called a couple. In a small dinghy, this heeling movement is counteracted partly by the natural stability of the hull, and partly by the crew moving their weight to hold the boat upright.

Most sailing dinghies have a jib as well as a mainsail (Figure 9). This sail is controlled in the same way as the mainsail, but the two sails working together produce a greater force than one might expect. This is because the 'slot' between the two sails helps to speed up the airflow

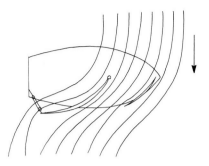

Figure 9. The combined effect of jib and mainsail

without making it turbulent, and so the 'pull' force is increased.

POINTS OF SAILING

So far, we have shown a boat sailing along with the wind blowing at right angles to the fore and aft line (on the beam), but a boat can sail in many other directions relative to the wind – indeed, sailing would be a pretty pointless pastime if it could not. For each point of sailing, as it is called, there is a correct way of setting the sail to get the maximum propulsion. The point of sailing we have studied so far, with the wind on the beam, is known as a beam reach.

Now let us imagine that the helmsman turns the boat a few degrees towards the direction from which the wind is blowing (luffing, Figure 10a). On this new course, the wind will no longer fill the sail properly, so it will start to lift unless the sheet controlling the sail is hardened in. (Figure 10b). Now the sail is once more drawing properly and driving the boat, but the change in the angle of the sail means that there is less force to drive the boat forward, and more force to make the boat heel. The crew will probably have to move outboard to balance the boat on this point of sailing, which is called a close reach.

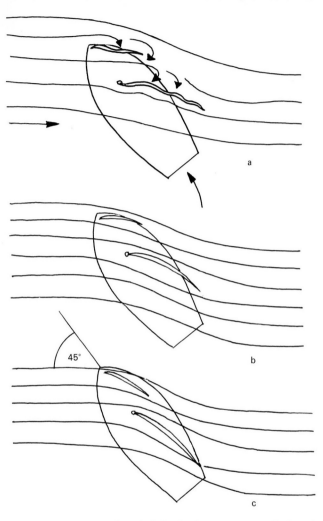

Figure 10 Luffing up into the wind. As the boat turns towards the wind, the sails will lift (*a*). They can be made to set properly again by taking in on the sheets (*b*). The limit comes with the boat at about 45° from the direction of the wind, with the sail hardened right in (*c*). The boat is said to be close-hauled

It is possible to continue this process of turning towards the wind, or luffing. Each time the sheet will need to be pulled in to make the sail set properly, and the driving force will decrease while the heeling force increases. The limit comes when the wind is about 45° on the bow, and the boom is more or less along the centreline of the boat (Figure 10c). The sail can be trimmed no further, and so any attempt to sail closer to the wind results in the sail lifting and loss of driving force. When a boat is sailing as close to the wind as possible, she is said to be close-hauled.

Now, let us return to the beam-reaching position of Figure 7b and consider what happens if we alter course the other way, away from the direction of the wind (bearing away, as it is called). If the helmsman bears away a few degrees, onto a broad reach (Figure 11a), the sail does not lift as when luffing, but it is now trimmed too flat, and the flow of air across it is not at its best. The sheets must be eased until the sail is once more just asleep. The driving force is restored, but because the boom is further out than it was, more of the force is available to drive the boat and less to make it heel. The boat sails faster, and in a more upright position. The limit to this process comes when the sheet is eased so far that the boom touches

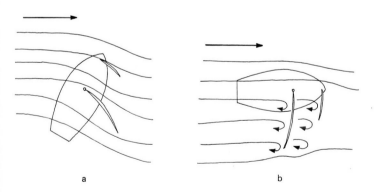

a   b

Figure 11. Bearing away from the wind. When turning away from the wind (*a*) the sheets must be eased to keep a smooth flow of wind over the sail. When the sheets are eased as far as they will go (*b*), the smooth flow is lost and the pull force disappears. The boat is said to be running

the shrouds holding up the mast. It can travel no further, so the sail is forced to remain where it is, destroying the smooth flow of air past it and hence eliminating the 'pull' force. The wind is coming from astern and the boat is said to be running (Figure 11b). Because the pull force has been lost, the boat does not travel as fast as on the reach, though the heeling force has disappeared. It may seem curious that a boat can go faster at an angle to the wind than it can with the wind behind it, but thanks to the power of the pull force, this is the case. Indeed, a high-speed sailing craft can reach at a speed greater than the speed of the wind, which is even more curious.

In Figures 10 and 11, we have seen how a boat can sail with the wind anywhere from 45° on the bow to right astern, and there must obviously be a similar set of points of sailing with the wind coming over the other side of the boat, or on the other tack. The tacks are named according to which side of the boat the wind comes over. Up to now, the boat has been on the port tack. If we were to arrange for the wind to come over the other side, she would be on the starboard tack (Figure 12). The next question is how to manoeuvre the boat from one tack to the other. There are two ways of doing this; the first is known as tacking, or going about, and starts with the boat close-hauled (Figure 13). To tack, the helmsman turns the boat firmly towards the direction of the wind by pushing the tiller down to leeward. The sails will immediately lift and lose drive, but if he times the manoeuvre correctly, the boat will have sufficient momentum to carry him round, through the eye of the wind and onto the other tack. When he has turned sufficiently far, the sails will fill again on the other side, and the boat will be sailing once more, but now close-hauled on the other tack.

The second way of going from one tack to the other is known as gybing (Figure 14). This time, the starting position is the run, with the boom out as far as it will go on one side. If the helmsman now turns the stern through the direction of the wind by pulling the tiller up to the weather side, a point will be reached when the wind

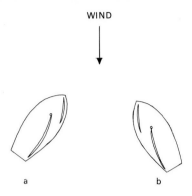

WIND

Figure 12. Tacks. If the wind comes over the port side of the boat (*a*), she is on the port tack. If the wind comes over the starboard side (*b*), she is on the starboard tack

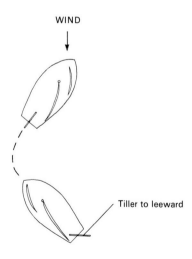

WIND

Tiller to leeward

Figure 13. Tacking – going from one tack to the other by turning the boat through the wind

29

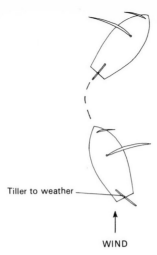

Tiller to weather

WIND

Figure 14. Gybing — going from one tack to the other by turning the stern through the wind

blows round onto the back of the sail, causing it to swing suddenly across the boat onto the other tack. Gybing is an operation that needs to be done with care, because the swinging boom can cause damage or injury if it is not properly controlled. Also it is quite easy when running to get the wind on the wrong side of the boat by mistake. This is called sailing by the lee, and it is dangerous because the boat could easily gybe unexpectedly, causing all sorts of havoc, possibly including a capsize. Both of these essential manoeuvres are described in further detail on pages 42 and 43 of Chapter 4.

Perhaps the best way to summarise this chapter is to have our imaginary helmsman sail his boat in a circle (Figure 15). He starts off close-hauled on the starboard tack, with the boat trying to heel quite markedly. He bears away, and at the same time eases the sheet to keep the sail properly trimmed. The boat speeds up and the heeling force is reduced. As he continues to bear away, he goes from close reach to beam reach to broad reach, until the boom is let out as far as it will go, and he finishes up on the run. He continues to turn until the boat gybes, and the boom swings across to the other side, and he is

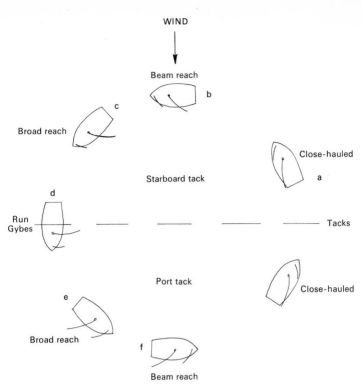

WIND

Beam reach
b

Broad reach
c

Close-hauled
a

Starboard tack

Run
Gybes
d

Tacks

Port tack

Close-hauled

Broad reach
e

Beam reach
f

Figure 15. Points of sailing

running on the other tack. Now he can gradually luff up, hardening in the sheet as he goes until he gets to the close-hauled position. Now, if he tacks, he will have returned to the point of sailing from which he started, having sailed full circle.

Provided the helmsman does not want to go in the sector in which the boat will not sail (ie within 45° of the direction of the wind), he can merely point the boat in the direction he wishes to go, trim the sails to suit, and all is well. If, however, he wants to go to some objective within the windward sector, he has to travel a zig-zag path, as shown in Figure 16. This process is called beating, or working to windward. It is important to keep the boat sailing as close to the wind as possible when beating, but

31

WIND

Figure 16. Beating, or working to windward. The boat must travel in a zig-zagging manner to reach an upwind objective, going from one tack to the other

without sailing so close that the sails stop working efficiently and the boat loses speed (pinching). This, together with all sorts of tactical decisions that need to be made when beating, makes the ability to sail a boat well to windward very hard to acquire, and much prized when it is achieved.

4 Boathandling

It is now time to put together all the information you have learned, and start sailing the boat. One problem for the newcomer is that once the boat is on the water, you cannot practise just one thing at a time. You cannot practise launching a boat, for example, without being able to recover it as well. If you practise running with the wind, then sooner or later you will have to turn round and beat back to your starting position. And while you can stop a car and get out and have a breather, the same thing is not so easy out on the water. So, your heart is likely to beat just a little faster the first time you take out your boat, though the prudent budding mariner will have taken a few lessons, and may even have spent a little time crewing for a friend.

TRAILING AND CAR-TOPPING

Unless you live very close to the place where you wish to sail, or keep your boat in a yacht club's dinghy park, you will first have to move your boat over the public roads from your home to the water's edge. If your boat is small and light enough, it can be carried on the roof of the car, which is in many ways easier, and more convenient than the alternative, a road trailer towed behind the car. The owner's handbook for the car will tell you the maximum weight that can be carried on the roof; when making the calculations, do not forget to add in the weight of the

The Ideal, designed by Jack Holt. A Plywood general purpose boat which can be easily assembled from a kit. A good family boat or basic trainer.

34

spars and of the roof rack itself. Tiny dinghies can be handled on and off the car single-handed. For bigger boats, two people are generally required, while three people can get a boat on or off a roof rack in seconds. An ordinary luggage rack on the roof is not suitable for carrying a boat. You need a ladder rack, which consists of two tubes running across the roof of the car. The boat should be carried upside down, with its side decks or gunwales supported on the tubes. Pad the support points carefully, and lash the boat firmly, so that it cannot move forwards, backwards or sideways, and cannot bounce up and down. Apart from the risk of damage, the police take a dim view of an insecure load and you may be prosecuted.

Driving with a boat on the roof is no problem; indeed, the shape of the boat seems in some cases to press the car more firmly onto the road, but bear in mind that the centre of gravity of the car has been raised, and you should accelerate, corner and brake with care. Also, you should be wary of high side winds, because the car and boat combination is much more sensitive to them than the car alone.

Trailing a boat behind a car is simple enough when going forward, though it becomes more interesting when you wish to back into a confined space. Reversing with a trailer is not easy at first, and you would do well to practise on some nice open space beforehand, so you can learn how to avoid jack-knifing. On the road, there are many regulations that need to be obeyed concerning the construction and lighting of the trailer, and the maximum speed allowed for towing. The boat must be properly secured to the trailer, and any part of the load which projects behind the trailer (such as the mast) must be properly marked. If you are intending to tow a boat on a trailer, make quite sure that you know and obey the rules. It is also important to make sure that the trailer fits the hull of the boat. A boat is designed to be supported evenly by the water, and is not constructed to resist concentrated loads on a small part of the hull. A badly fitting trailer, allied to the bumping received on the road, can easily cause severe damage.

Having arrived at the water's edge, it is not a good idea to put the road trailer into the water to launch the boat. The wheel bearings will get wet, and this can shorten their life. At the least, they will need re-packing with grease before they can be used on the road again. A better method of launching is to use a launching trolley, which will take no harm from a ducking; if you live near the water, or keep your boat in a dinghy park, then a launching trolley is almost essential. As with a road trailer, it is important that the chocks on the trolley fit the shape of the boat, or damage can be caused by the point loads on the hull. If you need to launch over a soft beach, then wide, inflated tyres are best.

THE WIND

When you arrive at the water, you need to consider the wind, which is the motive power of the boat. If there is no wind, the boat will make no progress; if there is too much wind, sailing will be uncomfortable or even dangerous. Look for other boats; if most boats around have reefed their sails or are threshing around in a welter of spray, then it might be better to stay where you are rather than risk meeting conditions for which you are not ready. Remember, also, that the shore gives shelter, and that winds tend to be stronger out at sea or in the middle of a large lake. The ideal breeze for a beginner is one that blows gently but steadily, putting ripples on the surface of the water but not raising little waves.

Once you get sailing, you will find that the wind is never constant for more than a few minutes. It varies both in speed and direction, and part of the art of sailing is to notice and make use of these variations. You should also be on the lookout for sudden and violent changes in the wind, which can sometimes happen. A squall or thunderstorm can bring strong winds which could cause a capsize if they took you unawares. Close to the coast or on rivers and lakes, hills, bays and headlands can deflect the wind so that its direction can vary suddenly. This can also be embarrassing, but you can usually spot such effects by looking at other boats or the way the wind blows on the water.

When reaching or running, it always appears that the wind is less than when beating, and what feels like a zephyr on the run can turn into a nasty sharp breeze when you turn round to come back; be careful about running off too far downwind, as the return may prove to be longer and more uncomfortable than you would like.

LAUNCHING

It is generally necessary to launch a dinghy from a beach or launching hard, and then recover it from the same place. You should first put the boat head to wind on the shore and rig it; then, with the sails lowered, wheel the boat on its launching trolley down into the water, until it floats off the trolley. The trolley should then be stowed away, ready for the return. In tidal water, put the trolley above the high water mark, or you may have to dive for it on your return. The long-suffering crewman then stands in the water, holding the boat head to wind, while the helmsman hoists the sails and makes sure that all is ready. The actual procedure for sailing away from the beach depends upon the direction of the wind; this may, of course, blow in any direction at all, but Figure 17 shows the three main possibilities.

Wind blowing along the shore When the helmsman is ready, the crewman pushes the bow of the boat out to sea, and climbs aboard bringing as little mud and water with him as he can manage. The helmsman hardens in the main sheet, and the boat sails off on a beam reach. When he has settled down, the crewman tends the jib, and pushes the plate or centreboard down when there is enough depth of water. The helmsman will similarly drop the rudder as the water deepens.

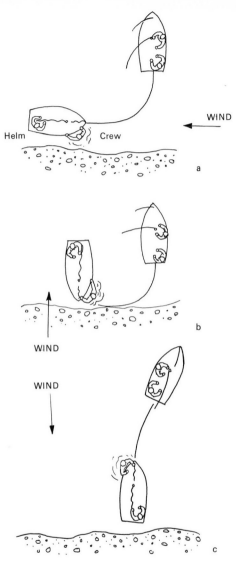

Figure 17. Launching from a beach
a Wind along the shore
b Weather shore
c Lee shore

38

Wind blowing off the shore (weather shore) This case is quite like the previous one; the crewman pushes the bow off and jumps in. However, as the boat will be running away from the beach, it will start to sail as soon as the boat is turned, so the crewman needs to be quick to avoid being left behind. The crewman then tends the jib sheet and the centreboard as before, while the helmsman lowers the rudder.

Wind blowing on the shore (lee shore)   The same principles apply as before, but the execution is rather more difficult. Firstly, the crewman holding the boat head to wind is necessarily in deeper water than in either of the previous situations. He must push the bow sharply whichever way the helmsman directs, then clamber in as quickly as possible, and get the jib set. The helmsman will have hardened the mainsheet right in, and will be attempting to sail off close-hauled but with no way on the boat and the rudder and centreboard both up, this is not easy to do. However, the worst that can happen is that the boat is blown ashore again, for the unfortunate crewman to leap over the side ready for another attempt.

RECOVERING

Bringing a boat back to the beach (recovering) is rather easier than taking it off, because the boat is already sailing and under control. As Figure 18 shows, there are again three main cases:

Wind blowing along the shore As the boat approaches the shore on a reach, the crewman lets fly the jib sheet, and prepares to lift the centreboard as the water shallows. The helmsman controls the speed of the boat by means of the mainsheet, eventually easing it right off to take the drive off the boat as the crewman steps out of the boat and holds it head to wind. The helmsman must not forget to raise the rudder as he comes in.

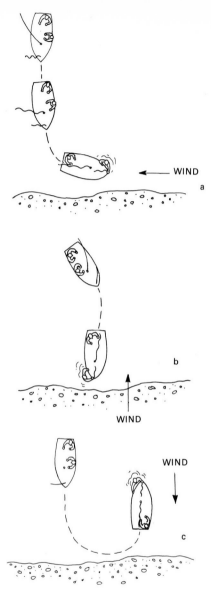

Figure 18. Returning to a beach
a Wind along the shore – reach in and luff head to wind
b Weather shore – approach close-hauled, then luff head to wind
c Lee shore – run in under jib or bare poles

40

Weather shore   In this case, the helmsman should approach the beach at an angle, close-hauled. As he gets near the beach, he should luff the boat head to wind, so judging matters that the boat stops just before it grounds (not easy at first). The crewman must look after the jib sheet until the helmsman tells him otherwise. As before, the centreboard and rudder must be raised as the water shallows.

Lee shore   The beach is approached on the run, and the problem is not so much getting there, but stopping when you arrive. Except in very light breezes, the best plan is to round up head to wind somewhere off shore and drop the mainsail; then run into the beach under the jib alone, letting the sheet fly (or dropping the sail) as the beach approaches. In very boisterous conditions, you may need to approach under bare poles, ie with no sail set at all.

JETTIES AND PONTOONS

Sailing away from a jetty or pontoon is very simple; arrange for the boat to lie head to wind while you rig it. When you are ready to go, put down the centreboard and rudder and get your crew to cast off and push the bow away until the sails fill on whichever tack you have chosen. If a tidal stream or current is running, use it to help you get clear, rather than letting it push you back onto the jetty.

When coming alongside a jetty, it is essential to stem the tide or current if one is flowing; reduce speed as you approach by letting the sheets fly or by dropping the sails. If there is no current, then come alongside as close to head wind as possible. The object is to bring the boat to rest a few inches away from the jetty, so your crew can grab it. Coming alongside neatly takes a lot of practice. It is far better to make several attempts cautiously than to crash headlong into the jetty, risking damage to your boat.

TACKING AND GYBING

In a small, una-rigged (that is, with only one sail) boat, tacking is no problem; the helmsman merely puts the helm down (to leeward), and as the boat swings through the eye of the wind, he moves from one side of the boat to the other, changing his hands on the tiller and the mainsheet as he does so. As the boat continues to turn, the sail will fill, and the helmsman then checks the turn with the rudder and gets the boat sailing again. He will find that he will be able to creep a little closer to the wind as the boat gathers speed. Gybing is almost as simple, except in very strong winds. As the stern of the boat passes through the wind's eye, the helmsman pulls in on the sheet to bring the boom across and as it swings over, he lets the sheet out again – important! The centreboard should be almost up when running to reduce resistance; if it is not, the boat can sometimes trip over the centreboard, leading to the risk of a capsize. A boat will also tend to fly up into the wind after a gybe, and this swing must be firmly checked with the rudder as the boom comes over.

With two people and two sails, going about is slightly more involved, as the crew must work as a team. The manoeuvre starts with the helmsman saying 'Ready about,' as a warning. Then, when all is ready, he says 'Lee-oh', as he puts the tiller to leeward. The boat will start to swing into the wind. As soon as the jib starts to lift, the crewman can let go of the sheet. As the boat comes into the wind, both he and the helmsman change sides, with the helmsman changing hands on the tiller and mainsheet. As the mainsail begins to fill on the new tack, the crewman should sheet in the jib to get the boat sailing as soon as possible.

When gybing, the helmsman gives warning 'Stand by to gybe', and then 'Gybe-oh' as he starts to turn. The crewman can drop the jib sheet (the jib is probably doing very little on the run anyway), and as the stern of the boat passes through the wind, he grasps the boom and shoves it over. The helmsman changes sides and hands, and the crewman changes sides as well, and begins to sort out the jib sheet. Both the crew should be ready to move out quickly if the boat shows any signs of excessive heel during or after the gybe. In very rough conditions it may be better to avoid gybing altogether, by going the long way round, that is by luffing up until close-hauled, tacking and then bearing away onto the new course.

PICKING UP A TOW

It is not uncommon for sailing dinghies to be offered a tow by a power boat. If the starting line for a club race is a long way from the launching hard, then the safety boat may tow competitors down to the start and back again after the race. If you get into difficulties, the safety boat will probably take you in tow, and if the wind falls light when you are a long way from home, a tow from a friendly passing motor boat can be very welcome.

The convention is that the boat being towed should provide the towing warp, but small sailing dinghies rarely carry anything suitable, so the motor boat has to tow with her own warp. The dinghy's painter is not usually suitable, because it is too thin, and it is made fast at the stemhead, where it cannot be let go in a hurry. The best place to make fast the warp is round the mast; make it fast with a slip hitch which can be undone instantly, or just wrap a few turns round the mast and hold the end. If you have to tow another boat behind you, then make the warp fast in the same way, either to your mast or to the thwart. A safety boat towing a lot of dinghies out for a race will often stream a long warp astern for boats to pick up and make fast to. When being towed, you should raise the centre-board and sit in the stern, so that the boat will follow easily, without the risk of sheering off and possibly capsizing. Follow the boat ahead closely; the golden rule is to aim your boat at the point of tow.

PICKING UP A MAN OVERBOARD

This is by no means a common emergency in sailing dinghies, where a capsize, leaving both crew in the water, is much more likely. Still, as it is possible, all helmsmen should know what to do; indeed, all crewmen should know as well, because it might be the helmsman who goes over the side.

The basic principle of picking up a man or other floating object is shown in Figure 19. Reach away from him with the wind on the beam while you get yourself sorted out; if you find that you cannot manage both jib and mainsail, then let the jib fly and raise the centreboard a little to improve the balance. Tack when ready, and reach back towards the man, spilling the wind from the sails as you approach by easing sheets. If you practise this operation, you will find that you have exact control over the boat's speed. Stop the boat with the man on your weather side, so you can grab hold of him and help him back into the boat.

WIND

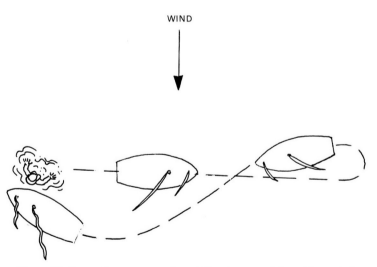

Figure 19. Recovering a man overboard. Reach away while getting sorted out, then tack and reach back. Control speed by easing sheets, and luff up with sheets eased to stop just to leeward

RIGHTING AFTER A CAPSIZE

Capsizes among racing dinghies are so common that it is not really correct to describe them as emergencies. A keen crew will press their boat to the limit for the sake of speed, and it is inevitable that they will misjudge the situation sooner or later and capsize. For the cruiser, a capsize might be more serious if there are young or inexperienced people on board, but by watching the weather, by reefing and by prudent seamanship, you can make a capsize very unlikely; it will always remain a possibility, though, perhaps caused by an error, or the breaking of some vital part like a toestrap. *All dinghy helmsmen and crew must know how to right their boat after a capsize.* And it is not enough to know merely the principles, given in Figure 20. All boats differ as to the ease with which they can be righted, and you should actually capsize your boat on purpose and then right her again. It is much easier to sort out your boat's own particular problems in warm, calm water, with someone keeping an eye on you than a mile off shore in a sharp little squall.

Figure 20.

a The boat has capsized and you are in the water. Don't climb onto the hull as this could cause the boat to invert. You must both swim to the stern, and then the helmsman checks that the rudder is intact, while the crew finds the end of the mainsheet.

b The crew gives the end of the mainsheet to the helmsman to use as a lifeline, and the helmsman swims to the centreboard. If the centreboard is in an up position, the helmsman steadies the boat while the crew swims in and pulls it down. The helmsman holds the centreboard to prevent the boat righting, or becoming inverted. Then the crew finds the jib sheet.

c The crew throws the jib sheet over the hull to the helmsman.

d The crew lies face forward in the water between the hull and boom. The submerged side deck will act as his support. He lets the helmsman know that he is ready.

46

e The helmsman climbs onto the centreboard, keeping his weight as close to the hull as is possible to avoid breaking the centreboard. The jib sheet can be used, if necessary, to provide extra leverage.

f The helmsman brings the boat upright by pulling on the jib sheet, and the crew will be tipped back into the boat with this motion.

g The crew helps the helmsman aboard. Be careful not to lean too far over, however, or you'll find that the balance of the boat is upset once more. Bail out the boat and you're on your way. If anything goes wrong, however, and you can't right the boat after a couple of tries, stay with the boat, and fire a distress flare.

TIDAL STREAMS

If you sail in the sea or in river estuaries, you should know something about the effects of tidal streams. The gravitational pull of the sun and the moon give rise to tides. The tide goes out and comes in twice a day in British waters, and the times of high water and low water, together with the range of the tide for the day, are given in tide tables. Every two weeks, the tides rise and fall to a greater extent than in the intervening weeks. When the range is large we have Spring tides, and when it is small, Neap tides. Spring tides occur shortly after full and new moon, and high water is in the early hours of the morning and soon after noon. The times of high water are often published in local newspapers, or on pocket cards which may be printed by local chandlers or shopkeepers, or by a yacht club.

It is important to know about the tides when sailing, because they affect the depth of water. For dinghies, this affects launching and recovery more than sailing about, because a dinghy draws only a few inches with the plate and rudder up and running aground has no terrors; all you have to do when the boat slides to a stop on the mud is to lift the plate and rudder and sail off. If, as sometimes happens, the boat is blown onto a lee shore and you cannot get it going before it grounds again, then you or your crew must hop out and shove the boat off; the only price you will pay will be a lot of mud in the bottom of the boat. For larger yachts, of course, grounding can be a serious matter.

But tides are not only important because of the depth of water, although high water can open up short cuts that are barred when the tide is low. As the water rises and falls, it also flows in and out, giving a horizontal movement to the surface. This horizontal movement is called a tidal stream, and is of the greatest importance in both cruising and racing tactics. You can get information about the tidal streams in a particular area by asking the locals or looking for yourself, or from charts or tidal stream atlases. The actual behaviour of a tidal stream depends upon the shape of the sea bottom, and it is possible to get some idea of how it will run by looking at a chart. The stream will run more strongly in a narrow strait or river, or around a headland, and less strongly into a bay. The direction of the flow is often modified by the coastline, and you may be set into a bay on the upstream side and set out of the bay at the other end; it is very likely that you will find a back eddy at the headland, which could be of decisive importance both for racing and cruising, if the tidal stream is strong and the wind is light.

RULE OF THE ROAD

Just as on land, there is a rule of the road at sea, to try to prevent ships colliding with each other. These rules have been internationally agreed, and are called the International Regulations for Preventing Collisions at Sea; the version in force at present was agreed in 1972. Strictly speaking, these rules only apply 'to all vessels upon the high seas and in all waters connected therewith', but the various local authorities responsible for inland waterways generally pass by-laws which impose the same rules on all boats.

The Collision Regulations, as the rules are often called, are lengthy and elaborate, but from the dinghy sailor's point of view become quite simple as he is unlikely to sail at night or in fog or to argue the toss with a supertanker.

The basic rules which apply to a sailing dinghy are as follows:

1 Always keep a lookout.
2 In narrow channels, keep to the starboard hand side.
3 If there is a risk that you might collide with another sailing boat, then act as shown in Figure 21. If you are on opposite tacks, then the boat on port tack gives way to the boat on starboard tack. If you are both on the same tack, then the boat to windward gives way.

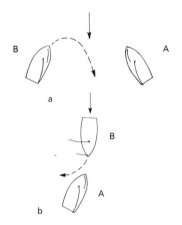

Figure 21. Collision rules — two sailing boats meeting
a Port tack — boat B keeps clear of starboard tack
b If on the same tack, the windward boat B keeps clear

4   If you are overtaking another boat, sail or power, you must keep clear.

5   A power driven vessel is supposed to keep clear of a sailing vessel, but the dinghy sailor would be wise not to insist on his rights too much; a motor yacht could be expected to keep clear of a sailing dinghy, but it is neither seamanlike nor good mannered to obstruct commercial shipping. Keep well clear, act in good time, and if in doubt head for shallow water where you will be safe. In fact, the old saying, 'steam gives way to sail' is now so hedged about with exceptions that you might be required to give way anyway.

Every dinghy sailor needs to master these simple rules, whether he goes cruising or racing. As we shall see in Chapter 6, different rules apply between boats racing (yet not between them and other water users). Racing rules, however, are based upon the Collision Regulations, and rule 3 above becomes of particular importance.

The International Fireball, designed by Peter Milne. A fast and exciting boat which can be built by an amateur. Sail numbers are over 12,000 world-wide.

The Mirror, designed by Jack Holt and Barry Bucknell. This very popular plywood kit boat has introduced tens of thousands of young people to sailing. Current sail numbers exceed 61,000.

5 Sailing Fast

Once you have learned the essentials of making a boat travel under sail, the next step is to refine the technique in order to get the best possible performance from the boat. When racing, this quest for speed is obviously essential if you are to have any chance of winning; but the cruising man needs to be able to sail efficiently as well – that little extra speed may mean all the difference between missing a tide or losing a dying breeze, and consequently spending much longer on a passage than is necessary. If sailors have a watchword, it is 'the sooner the better'. Anything that needs doing should be done at once, and as quickly as possible, because you can never predict what is going to happen next.

SAIL TRIMMING

In Chapter 3, we saw that when close-hauling or reaching, the maximum force to drive the boat appeared when the flow of air across the sail was smooth. This happens when the sail is sheeted in until it just fills evenly all over, or 'goes to sleep'. For a una-rigged boat, sail trimming merely consists of ensuring that the sheet is adjusted to this point at all times, but when a jib and mainsail are set together the situation is more complicated because the two sails interact with each other. The helmsman and his crew must work together to get the best result. First the mainsail should be sheeted correctly, followed by the jib. This will almost certainly cause the mainsail to lift, as the flow of air from the jib backwinds it. The mainsail should be adjusted again, and a final check made on the jib. With a little experience, the whole process takes only seconds. As the wind is constantly varying in both strength and direction, the crew should be continuously aware of the need to check the trim of the sails, especially the jib. Tiny streamers of wool attached near the luff of the sail can help to show that the airflow is smooth. When the sail is properly set, the wools on both sides lie horizontal; if the wool on the weather side starts to lift, the sheet needs to be hardened in, and if the wool on the lee side lifts, the sheet should be eased. In the long run, boat speed depends mainly upon sail trim, and races are more often won by good sail trimming than by anything else.

CONTROLLING THE SHAPE OF THE SAIL

The shape of the sail can be altered by the way it is set to suit differing conditions; in general, light winds call for a full sail, and stronger winds need a much flatter sail. High performance boats are able to control sail shape by a variety of methods, but unless handled by an expert, they can often do more harm than good. Only the more simple techniques are discussed below.

The halyard   For a jib, especially when close-hauled, it is vital to have as straight a luff as possible, so the jib halyard should be set up tightly. For a mainsail, it is possible to set up the halyard so that luff of the sail is fairly slack in light winds, though it should be tight in fresh winds. The resulting vertical crease will be blown out by the pressure of the wind.

The clew outhaul   This enables the clew to be hauled out towards the end of the boom in stronger winds, flattening the curve in the foot of the sail.

53

The kicking strap   When a boat is sailing off the wind with the main sheet eased, the boom tends to lift. If it is allowed to do so, the sail develops a twist, which means that it cannot be set correctly all the way up. The kicking strap prevents this twist from becoming excessive (Figure 22).

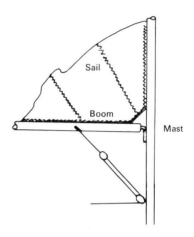

Figure 22. A kicking strap is used to control sail twist by preventing the boom from lifting

Main sheet position   Whilst not strictly an adjustment, there are two possible ways of fixing the main sheet to the boom. In boats intended mainly for cruising, the sheet is fixed to the end of the boom, where it is out of the way. In many racing boats, the sheet is fixed somewhere near the middle of the boom, with the other end of the purchase on a track in the boat (see Figure 23). This allows for the independent control of twist and the position of the boom relative to the centreline. The advantages of this arrangement are most clearly seen in windward work.

Cunningham tackle   The cunningham tackle is a way of tensioning the luff of the mainsail (and sometimes the jib). The sailmaker cuts a small belly in the foot of the sail, to give good flow in light winds; the cunningham effectively 'reefs' this belly, to flatten the sail for stronger

54

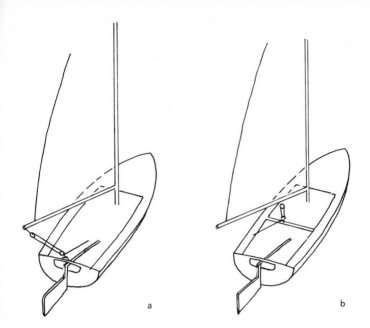

Figure 23. Alternative main sheet arrangements
a In simple boats, the mainsheet is usually led from the end of the boom to a horse across the transom
b In more powerful racing boats, the mainsheet is often fixed to the middle of the boom and a traveller which moves across the centre of the boat

winds. An eye is sewn into the luff of the sail, a few inches above the tack. A line is passed through the eye and used to pull down on the luff, putting in extra tension to flatten the sail.

KEEPING THE BOAT UPRIGHT

As we saw in Chapter 3, the wind produces a heeling force, as well as a driving force, which limits the power that can be applied to a boat. If the crew are better able to counteract the heeling force, then the boat can be driven harder.

Toestraps With toestraps, the crew can sit further out with confidence and relative comfort (see Figure 24).

55

It is important to site the toestraps correctly; they should catch the instep almost automatically when sitting on the side deck. Make sure that they are firmly attached to the boat, because a broken toestrap can lead to man overboard and a capsize, both at once!

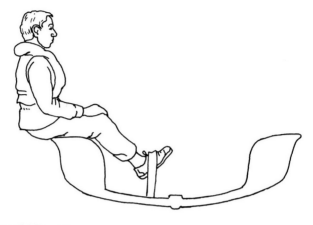

Figure 24. Toestrap

Trapeze The trapeze is a wire attached well up the mast. The crewman attaches this wire to a special harness, and he can then place his entire body weight outside the boat, to keep it up (Figure 25). He can now exert considerable control over the heel of the boat, for good or ill, depending upon his experience. The helmsman is confined to the boat by the need to hold the tiller extension so he sits out with toestraps.

THE SPINNAKER

The spinnaker is a large, light sail set to increase the power of the boat when running or reaching – its usefulness usually disappears by the time the wind is on the beam, because the heeling force gets larger than the crew can handle. There is a tendency among newcomers to think of the spinnaker as a complicated and dangerous sail,

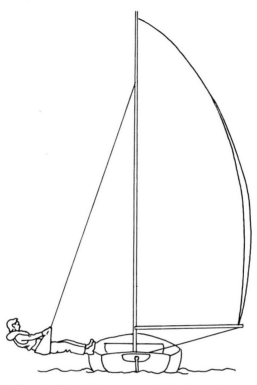

Figure 25. The principle of the trapeze, which allows the crew to get his weight further outboard, thus increasing the righting force

but if it is handled properly, it makes for fast and exhilarating sailing. On the other hand, there is no doubt that if the spinnaker gets out of control, it can be a very considerable embarrassment. As with all aspects of sailing, the secret of good spinnaker work is practice, with your own boat and crew. Each class of dinghy has different problems, and you can to some extent choose the gear and drill for setting and handling a spinnaker yourself, so the following paragraphs can do no more than outline the basic principles. Set your spinnaker first on the run, on a quiet day and then play around with it until you and your crew are confident that you can master the sail.

One of the complications with a spinnaker is that there

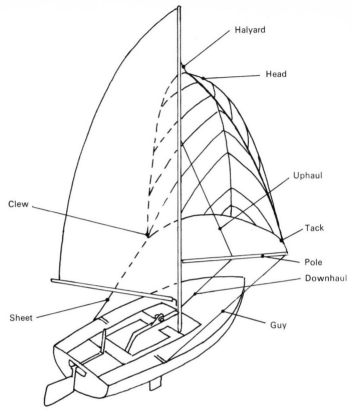

Figure 26. The general arrangement of the spinnaker

are suddenly about twice as many ropes to play with as there were before. Figure 26 shows the general arrangement of a spinnaker. The sail is hoisted by a halyard, and is controlled by two other ropes, one at each corner. The leeward one is the sheet, and is attached to the clew of the spinnaker; the windward rope is called a guy, and is attached to the tack of the spinnaker. The spinnaker pole which holds the luff of the spinnaker to windward, is also attached to the tack. A confusing thing about the spinnaker is that it is symmetrical. On the other tack, the previous luff becomes the new leach, the old sheet becomes the new guy, and so on. There is no physical change (except that the pole is moved across) – it is only the names that change, not the ropes themselves.

There are two other ropes of importance in spinnaker work; the spinnaker pole is controlled by an uphaul (or topping lift) and a downhaul, so that the pole can be held steady in any desired position. In some boats, it is also possible to move the heel of the pole up or down the mast.

When the boat is running before the wind, the spinnaker merely intercepts a lot of wind, which helps to push the

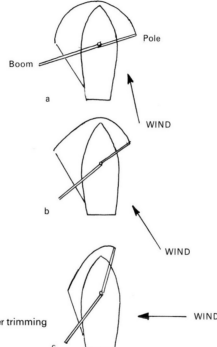

Figure 27. Spinnaker trimming
a Running
b Broad reaching
c Close reaching

boat along, but on other points of sailing it is possible to trim the spinnaker to get something of a flow across it, thus giving rise to a 'pull' force as well. The proper trimming of a spinnaker will only be learned by experience, but the basic principles are simple enough (Figure 27):

59

1 The pole should be adjusted so that the tack and the clew of the spinnaker are the same height. If the heel of the pole can be moved, then the pole should also be horizontal, to take the stresses better.

2 The guy should be set so that the pole and the main boom are in line with each other, the boom abaft the mast to leeward and the pole forward and to weather.

3 The sheet should be set so that the luff of the spinnaker is just about to curl. If it does begin to collapse, then a sharp tweak on the sheet, followed by a gentle ease, will restore the situation. In light weather, if the sheet is too tight or the pole too far forward, the sail may collapse from the leach.

These three simple rules will not give you the best possible trim for your spinnaker, but they do guarantee that the sail will set and draw, so that you can experiment by degrees to get the best out of it.

SETTING A SPINNAKER

The essential point to remember when trying to sort out the welter of spinnaker gear is that the *spinnaker sets outboard of everything*. The sail itself is carried forward of the forestay, and the sheet and guy lead outside the shrouds. There are many possible ways of setting the spinnaker, but for the beginner it is easiest to hoist it to leeward, under the foot of the jib. This means that the sail will be blanketed by the other sails until it is almost right up, and there is less chance of it getting out of control.

The first step is to flake the sail (ie, stow it in such a way that it will come out again without twists or tangles) into its bag or bucket. You would, of course, make sure that this had been done before a race, but you may well want to set the spinnaker several times during the course of a race. Put the foot in first, and then feed the sail in carefully, making sure that there are no twists in it; follow up the coloured tapes sewn on each side of the sail with your fingers. Then lay the container ready, with the three corners exposed. They are normally marked red and green, for port and starboard, and blue for the head. The next steps are as follows:

1 The halyard is taken to leeward of the forestay outside the jib and led under the foot of the jib to the spinnaker head.

2 The sheet is led from its fairlead aft, outside the shrouds to the appropriate corner of the spinnaker.

3 The guy is led along the weather side from its fairlead, outside the shrouds and the forestay to the other corner of the sail.

4 As the helmsman hoists the sail, the crewman rigs the pole between the tack and the mast, and fits the pole uphaul and downhaul to the clip on the pole.

5 As soon as the helmsman has made the halyard fast to its cleat and sees that the pole is in place, he can set the pole to the right angle with the guy, and then cleat the guy.

6 The crewman can then take the sheet and start to trim the sail. A lot of minor adjustments will probably be needed to get the best possible set.

Among the many possible variations to this drill are setting the sail from the windward side or rigging the pole before hoisting. In this case, the guy itself is dropped through the fitting at the end of the pole, running freely through it. This arrangement is of advantage when setting the spinnaker on the reach, when the boat could easily be over-pressed if the crewman has to fiddle with the pole after hoisting the spinnaker, rather than sitting out at once.

THE SPINNAKER CHUTE

The spinnaker chute is becoming very popular, even in boats much bigger than dinghies, as it allows for very easy setting and handing of the spinnaker, at the price of a rather large hole in the foredeck. The arrangement is shown in Figure 28. The halyard leads from the head of the sail to the cleat, and then through the chute to a reinforced patch in the middle of the sail. Hoisting is simplicity itself. As the helmsman hoists, the crewman clips on the pole as the tack comes clear of the chute, and both the crew then proceed to trim the sail as before. To hand (that is, to take in) the spinnaker, the pole is removed and the sheet and guy hardened in to fold the spinnaker around the forestay. The helmsman lets off the halyard and hauls in on the retrieving line; as soon as the middle of the sail is well into the chute, the sheet and guy are let go. The head should enter last.

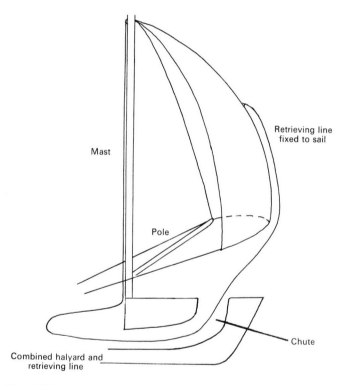

Figure 28. A spinnaker chute

HANDING THE SPINNAKER

On a run, the crewman can take off the pole and gather the tack and the clew in his arms. Then, as the helmsman lowers the sail, he can drop it straight into its container ready for the next hoist. On a reach, with the sail full of wind, a different approach is needed. The crewman holds onto the sheet, while the helmsman lets the guy right off so that it runs out through the end of the pole. The sail will collapse behind the main, and the crewman can gather it in as the helmsman lowers away. For this technique to work, the guy must be able to run loosely through the end of the pole, and this 'loose guy' rig is probably the best to adopt as a standard drill.

GYBING THE SPINNAKER

The only safe way for a newcomer to gybe a spinnaker is from one run to the other; experts can gybe smartly from one reach to the other, but the violent changes in trim that are needed will lead the beginner to disaster. If you require the gybe from one reach to the other, then bear away to a run, then gybe, then luff up to the reach. The procedure for gybing the spinnaker on the run is as follows:

1   The crewman unhooks the pole from the mast and hooks it onto the sheet. The pole now spans the sail from tack to clew.
2   He then unhooks the pole from the guy, and attaches it to the mast. Hey presto – the spinnaker is gybed!

The only minor problem to be worked out in this manoeuvre is that the mainsail must also be gybed at some point in the proceedings.

BROACHING

Broaching is an uncontrollable swing into the wind which can occur when close reaching under spinnaker. The boat swings into wind, heels over sharply, and will almost inevitably capsize. After a very early stage, the broach is uncontrollable because the rudder comes out of the water. The prevention (for there is no cure) of this condition is to keep the boat upright at all costs, and if the boat shows signs of heeling, then bear away and ease sheets.

On spinnaker work in general, it is inevitable that sooner or later (probably sooner), you will get into the most embarrassing muddle. This will cause the rest of the fleet considerable merriment, but do not despair; their turn will come!

PLANING

If a light racing dinghy can be made to go fast enough, which requires sufficient wind in the right quarter and accurate sail trimming, then it can be made to ride up on its own bow-wave and skim over the surface, rather than displacing water as it generally does. The result is a dramatic increase in speed for as long as the right conditions persist. This may be only for a few seconds, as a puff accelerates the boat, or it can last for some time in a strong, steady wind. For planing it is essential that the boat be more or less upright, the crew weight should be aft, and the centreboard should be up. There are two ways in which you can attempt to get the boat on the plane:

1 Wait for a gust, move aft smartly, and at the same time harden in the sheets.
2 If the boat is sailing on the limit of control with the crew as far out as they can go, then bear away and ease sheets when the gust comes. As the boat gets on the plane, edge it back onto course.

The International Enterprise, designed by Jack Holt. A fast and enjoyable racing boat which can also be cruised or sailed by the family. Available in wood or GRP.

6 Racing

Having mastered the sailing of your boat and practised the skills for making it go as fast as possible, you will probably want to try out yourself and your boat against others. Although many dinghy sailors are content to cruise around on their own, the pressure and excitement of racing has great appeal, and if you are not dedicated to full-time racing you can always combine it with your cruising, to give a varied pattern to your sailing. You can, for example, race on one day of the weekend and cruise on the other, or, if you live close enough to your club, you may be able to race on weekday evenings and keep your weekends free for some other form of sailing.

Racing is organised by clubs, so the first thing you need to do is to join a suitable club. In choosing a club, you must obviously pick one in an area near your home, and with the type of water you like to sail in – lake, reservoir, river or sea. You should also pick a club which organises races for your class of dinghy, so that you will have a number of other sailors to compete against, all with more or less the same type of boat. In this way, you can really judge your ability in sailing. If this turns out to be difficult or impossible, then many clubs arrange handicap races. Any class of dinghy can take part in these races, and the time that each takes to complete the race is adjusted by a proportion depending upon its Portsmouth Yardstick Rating. The Portsmouth Yardstick is a scheme administered by the Royal Yachting Association, to allow boats of different performance to race against each other.

Handicap racing is less immediate than class racing, because you may not know how well you did until some time after the event, when the race organisers have had a chance to work out the results. It is particularly useful for the person who races only occasionally, because it means that he can choose the dinghy he wants to buy without worrying too much about what the other members of his club have bought. For the dedicated racing man, however, the choice of dinghy and the choice of club go hand in hand.

Dinghy races consist of several laps around a course (Figure 29). The start and finish lines are formed by bringing in line two objects, such as poles on shore or the start boat and a buoy on the water. The turning marks are generally buoys laid for the purpose by the club; as often as not they are orange in colour and marked with a flag to make them easier to see. The race starts at a pre-arranged time, and warning signals are given ten and five minutes before the start. At ten minutes, the class flag is hoisted and some sound signal is made, such as a gun or hooter. Five minutes before the start, the preparatory flag is hoisted (International Code Flag P) and another sound signal made. At the start, both the class flag and the preparatory flag are lowered, again with a sound signal. As guns or hooters have been known to go wrong, you should remember that the flag signal is the one that counts, not the sound signal; and if you are using the sound signal because you happen to be a long way from the starting point, remember that sound travels relatively slowly, so your time may be a second or two wrong if the sound has had a distance to travel.

Sailing races are controlled by flags, and you should find out what the various flags look like and what they mean. The most important signals are as follows:

'Answering pendant'	Postponement signal
'Code Flag B'	Protest flag (flown by a yacht)
'Code Flag L'	Flown ashore; a notice to competitors has been posted on the notice board

Blue Flag	Finishing signal, displayed by a committee boat on station at the finishing line
'Code Flag M'	Mark signal; round or pass the object showing this flag instead of the mark it replaces
'Code Flag N'	All races are abandoned
'Code Flag P'	Preparatory signal
'Code Flag S'	Shorten course signal
'First Substitute'	General recall signal
Red Flag	Leave all marks to port
Green Flag	Leave all marks to starboard

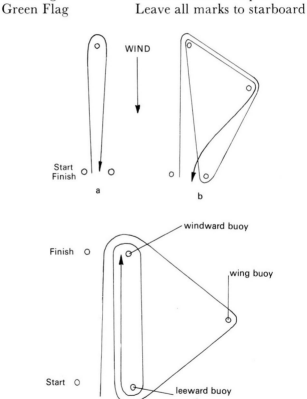

Figure 29. Typical courses. c is known as an Olympic course, and the start is always to windward

Preparation for a race begins some time before the start. The first thing to do after you have decided to enter is to find out when and how you should enter, and pay any entrance fee that may be required. Make sure that you know the day and the time of your start. It is irritating enough to arrive at the line ten minutes late because you have got the time of the start wrong. It is even more irritating to arrive on the wrong day – but it happens!

On the day itself, arrive early (with your crew, if you have one), and read and digest the race instructions minutely. These contain vital information such as the time of the various signals, the course to be sailed, the number of laps and much else besides. Then rig your boat slowly and carefully, and make sure that everything is there and in working order. Once the gun goes, you will want your boat to be on top line, so make most of those last-minute adjustments well before the race. Then launch your boat and sail around as fast as you can, to get the feel of the boat in the particular conditions of wind and sea that exist. This is the time for you to adjust such things as the shape of the sail and the positions of the sheet leads (if your class rules allow you to adjust these). If you can, sail round the course to ensure that you can sail your boat to its best advantage on each leg. Look out for the peculiarities like a back-eddy in the current or a wind shadow, which you can turn to advantage over less well prepared competitors. However, bear in mind that most clubs run very full programmes of races, and you must make certain that you do not interfere in any way with boats which may be racing. The whole object of this warm-up is to get yourself, your crew, and your boat working like a well-oiled machine before you start driving it to the limit.

With the large fleets that are common nowadays, the start can be very unnerving for the beginner. Most race committees try to arrange for a windward start if possible, so that the first leg of the course is a beat. In the moments before the start, therefore, boats are zigzagging wildly in the vicinity of the line, all jockeying for position, and

trying to ensure that their boat hits the line at the instant
of the start going at full speed and generally on the starboard tack, because as we shall see, starboard tack
boats have right of way over port tack boats. In the
period between the ten minute gun and the start, you
should decide what you want to do. It is unusual for
the race committee to get the line exactly where they want
it, so you may find that there are a few yards advantage
in starting at one end or the other. But this bias on the
line will attract all the other competitors as well, so you
might be better off at the other end, or in the middle, with
fewer dinghies around and a clear wind. For the newcomer, this is by far the best approach; keep your wind
clear. Not only is it much less worrying, but you will gain
in boat speed and freedom to manoeuvre. Fighting with
the pack takes strong nerves, and it is only the helmsmen
who get it exactly right who really benefit.

RULES OF RACING

At the start, and indeed for five minutes beforehand,
the rules of racing will have been in force, so let us
examine them. Yacht races, for boats of all sizes are sailed
under a set of internationally agreed rules, the International Yacht Racing Union Rules, which are administered in Britain by the Royal Yachting Association. The
rules explained in this book are the 1977 edition. Changes
to rules are made from time to time, but as far as the
ordinary weekend racers are concerned, these changes are
unlikely to have much effect, as they are generally only
important in the upper strata of yacht competition where
money and national pride start to matter. In ordinary
terms, the rules have operated satisfactorily over many
years and are likely to remain as they are. Dinghy racing
is like any other sport in that the competitor who does not
know the rules is unlikely to win, even if he does not foul
an opponent through his own ignorance; learn the rules –
the full rules, and not this short summary.

As far as possible the wording of the International

Yacht Racing Rules has been used, but the actual rules are worded rather more fully than these extracts, to cover every situation.

First a few definitions:

Racing   A yacht is racing from her preparatory signal until she has either finished and cleared the finishing line and finishing marks or retired or until the race has been postponed, abandoned or cancelled.

Starting   A yacht starts when after her starting signal, any part of her hull, crew or equipment first crosses the starting line in the direction of the course to the first mark.

Finishing   A yacht finishes when any part of her hull, or of her crew or equipment in normal position, crosses the finishing line from the direction of the course from the last mark.

Luffing   Altering course towards the wind until head to wind.

Tacking   A yacht is tacking from the moment she is beyond head to wind until she has borne away, when beating to windward, to a close-hauled course; if not beating to windward, to the course on which her mainsail has filled.

Bearing away   Altering course away from the wind until a yacht begins to gybe.

Gybing   A yacht begins to gybe at the moment when, with the wind aft, the foot of her mainsail crosses her centre line, and completes the gybe when the mainsail has filled on the other tack.

On a tack   A yacht is on a tack when she is not tacking or gybing. A yacht is on the tack (starboard or port) corresponding to her windward side.

Close-hauled   A yacht is close-hauled when sailing by the wind as close as she can lie with advantage in working to windward.

Clear astern and clear ahead; overlap   A yacht is clear astern of another when her hull and equipment in normal position are abaft an imaginary line projected abeam from the aftermost point of the other's hull and equipment in normal position. The other yacht is clear ahead. The yachts overlap when neither is clear astern; or if, although one is clear astern, an intervening yacht overlaps both of them. The terms clear astern, clear ahead and overlap apply to yachts on opposite tacks only when they are subject to Rule 42 (Rounding or Passing Marks and Obstructions). See Figure 30.

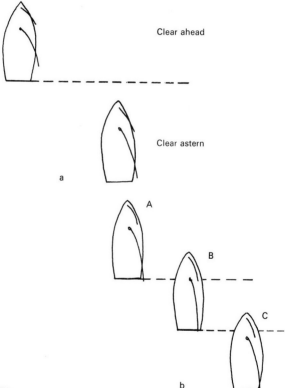

Figure 30.
a Clear ahead and clear astern
b Overlapping boats. C has an overlap on A because of B, an intervening yacht

Leeward and windward   The leeward side of a yacht is that on which she is (or if luffing head to wind, was), carrying her mainsail. The opposite side is the windward side (Figure 31*a*). When neither of two yachts on the same tack is clear astern, the one on the leeward side of the other is the leeward yacht. The other is the windward yacht (Figure 31*b*).

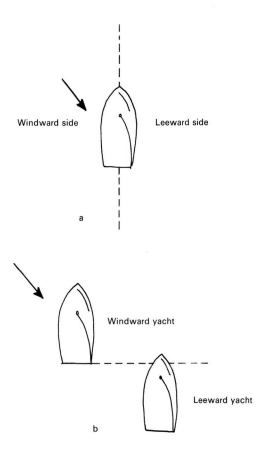

Figure 31. Windward and leeward

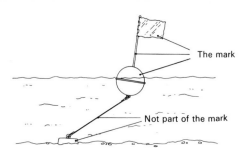

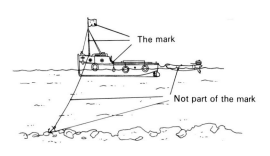

Figure 32. Marks of the course

Proper course A proper course is any course which a yacht might sail after the starting signal, in the absence of the other yacht or yachts affected, to finish as quickly as possible. There is no proper course before the starting signal.

Mark A mark is any object specified in the sailing instructions which a yacht must round or pass on a required side. Every ordinary part of a mark ranks as part of it, including a flag, flagpole, boom or hoisted boat, but excluding ground tackle and any other object either accidentally or temporarily attached to the mark. See Figure 32.

Obstruction   An obstruction is any object, including a vessel under way, large enough to require a yacht, when not less than one overall length away from it, to make a substantial alteration of course to pass one side or the other. An obstruction is also any object which can be passed on one side only, including a buoy when the yacht in question cannot safely pass between it and the shoal or object which it marks. See Figure 33.

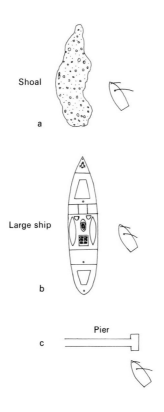

Shoal

a

Large ship

b

Pier

c

Figure 33. Examples of obstructions

The above definitions (and some others) form Part 1 of the rules. Part 2 is concerned with the management of races and the duties of the Race Committee, and Part 3 deals with the responsibilities of the owner of a yacht. Part 4 gives the right of way rules, which are those which most immediately concern a person racing. It begins on a stern note: yachts which infringe rules may be disqualified or penalized for infringing the rules, and for seriously hindering another yacht which is racing, even if she is not racing herself. A yacht which realises that she has infringed a racing rule or a sailing instruction is obliged to retire or accept an alternative penalty if the sailing instructions allow this. And yachts with the right of way have obligations, too. If such a yacht fails to take reasonable steps to avoid a collision resulting in serious damage, she may be disqualified as well as the offender; and if she makes an alteration of course which might not be foreseen by the other yacht and a collision involving serious damage occurs, she may be disqualified if she did not hail the other yacht first, to warn of her intentions (there is an important exception to this rule in Rule 38.1, Luffing and Sailing above a Proper Course after Starting, which is explained later). The right of way yacht is also forbidden to alter course so as to prevent the other yacht from keeping clear.

RIGHT OF WAY RULES

The basic right of way rules in yacht racing are based on the International Regulations for Preventing Collisions At Sea, but much extended and codified.

Opposite tack – basic rule A port tack yacht shall keep clear of a starboard tack yacht (Figure 34).

Same tack – basic rules
1   When overlapped: a windward yacht shall keep clear of a leeward yacht.
2   When not overlapped: a yacht clear astern shall keep clear of a yacht clear ahead. See Figure 35.

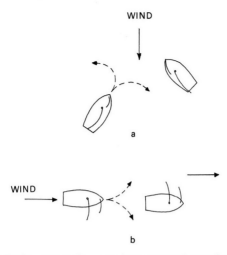

WIND

a

WIND

b

Figure 34 Opposite tacks — a yacht on port tack must keep clear of a yacht on starboard

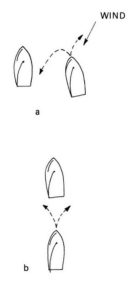

WIND

a

b

Figure 35. Same tacks — when overlapped the windward yacht must keep clear. If there is no overlap an overtaking yacht must keep clear

77

3   Transitional: a yacht which establishes an overlap
    to leeward from clear astern shall allow the windward
    yacht ample room and opportunity to keep clear.

**Same tack – luffing and sailing above a proper
course after starting**   Luffing is one of the most
common racing tactics used when attempting to prevent
another yacht overtaking. The IYRU rules are rather
difficult to understand for the newcomer, so the basic
principles of luffing are given here in less formal language.
To master the full implications of luffing, you will of course
have to go back to the rules themselves.

The basic principles of luffing are described in Figure
36. When a yacht tries to overtake another on the same
tack, she can either do so to windward or to leeward. If
possible, she would like to do so to windward, because she
keeps her own wind clear, and eventually puts the over-
taken yacht in her wind shadow, causing it to slow down.
The yacht ahead, on the other hand, would prefer the
overtaking yacht to come to leeward, because then the
faster boat will get the wind shadow and may not be able
to overtake at all. So, relying on the first two basic rules
for yachts on the same tack, the yacht ahead can luff (as
far as head to wind if she wishes), thus preventing the
yacht astern and to windward from overtaking as he is
obliged to keep clear either by falling behind again or by
luffing with the leeward yacht. She may even have to tack
if luffed head to wind. The yacht ahead or to leeward
can luff as much and as often as she wishes without
warning, until the overtaking yacht manages to break
through – if she can. With the boats on parallel courses, if
the helmsman of the windward boat, sitting in his normal
position, sees the mast of the other yacht abeam of him,
he can hail 'Mast abeam'. At this moment, the leeward
yacht's luffing rights disappear, and she must immediately
return to the proper course (or sail below it). There are
some further limitations on luffing; an overlap is not
considered to exist unless the yachts are within two
lengths of each other, and if there is more than one yacht

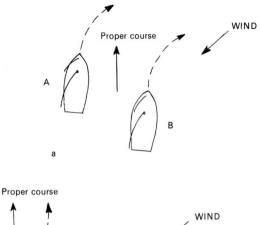

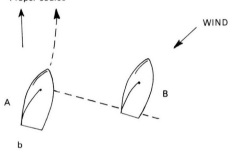

Figure 36. Luffing
a Boat A may luff B as far as head to wind, without warning. B must keep clear
b When B sees A's mast abeam, she hails 'Mast abeam'. Boat A must return immediately to the proper course

to windward, the leeward yacht may not luff unless she has luffing rights over *all* the yachts which will be affected by the luff. Subject to these limitations, a windward yacht must respond to the luff unless an obstruction of some kind prevents her from doing so. In such a case she should hail the leeward yacht, asking for water at the obstruction.

Luffing according to this rule is only allowed after the start. Before the start, a yacht may luff slowly, giving the windward yacht ample opportunity to keep clear. She should not luff above a close-hauled course unless the other helmsman is abaft her mainmast.

Luffing is a useful manoeuvre, but it has greater value as a threat than as a tactic. In a luff, both yachts lose ground and may let a third competitor slip past them both. The mere threat of a luff is generally sufficient to ensure that a faster boat will overtake to leeward, though you should always be ready to defend your rights if someone tries to take you to windward. Bear in mind, too, that if a yacht does overtake to leeward and in the process gets more than two lengths away from you, she has luffing rights over you if she closes you again.

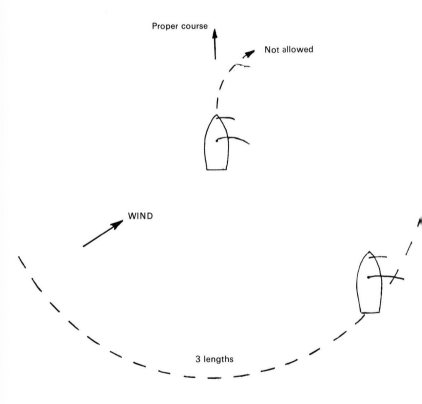

Figure 37. Same tack – sailing below a proper course. This is not allowed if a yacht is within three lengths and trying to overtake to leeward

Same tack – sailing below a proper course after starting   A yacht which is on a free leg of the course shall not sail below her proper course when she is clearly within three of her overall lengths of either a leeward yacht or a yacht clear astern which is steering a course to pass to leeward – see Figure 37. The purpose of this rule is to prevent a windward yacht bearing down on another to stop it getting past.

Changing tacks – tacking or gybing
1   A yacht which is tacking or gybing shall keep clear of a yacht on a tack.
2   A yacht shall neither tack nor gybe into a position which will give her right of way unless she does so far enough from a yacht on a tack to enable this yacht to keep clear without having to begin to alter her course until after the tack or gybe has been completed.
3   When two yachts are both tacking or gybing at the same time, the one on the other's port side shall keep clear.

The purpose of this rule is, for example, to stop a yacht tacking onto starboard under the nose of an opponent without giving him time to give way.

Rounding marks and obstructions   The rules change when yachts get close to a turning mark or other obstruction. As it is here that yachts tend to bunch up, every helmsman must have the rules which apply at his fingertips. Figure 38 illustrates the rules.

The basic rule says that an outside yacht shall give each yacht overlapping her on the inside, room to round or pass the mark or obstruction. Room includes room for an overlapping yacht to tack or gybe when either is an integral part of the manoeuvre. The overlap must be established at least two boats lengths away from the mark, and the outside yacht must still give water to an inside one if she manages to break the overlap inside this distance. With the wind free, it does not matter which tack the inside yacht is on, but if the yachts are beating up to the mark, or if one must tack round it, then the port

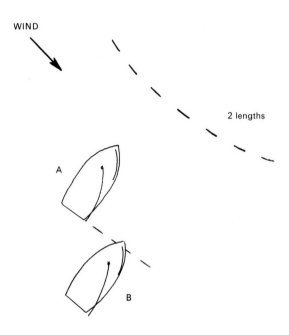

WIND

2 lengths

A

B

Figure 38. B has established an overlap more than two boats lengths from the mark, so A must give her room to round the mark

tack yacht must keep clear, even if an overlap has been established.

The rules relating to rounding a mark are particularly complex, as it is here that the majority of close encounters take place. If newcomers follow the basic rules above, they should keep out of trouble, but it is only with experience and detailed study of the rules that a helmsman can extract the maximum advantage from the confused situations that are likely to occur.

There is an exception to the basic rule at the start. When approaching the line, a leeward yacht is not obliged to give a windward yacht room to pass to leeward of a starting mark (provided there is navigable water around it). But after the starting signal, the leeward yacht must not sail above the proper course or above close-hauled.

Close-hauled – hailing for room to tack at an obstruction It may happen that when two yachts are on the same tack, the yacht ahead or the leeward yacht may have to tack to avoid some obstruction. If she cannot tack without colliding with the other yacht, then she shall hail the other yacht for room to tack, but must not hail and tack simultaneously. In reply to this hail, the other yacht has two courses open to it; she can tack, in which case the hailing yacht must tack at the earliest moment that she can clear the hailed yacht. Or, if she thinks that she can keep clear without tacking, she can hail 'You tack', or words to that effect. In this case, the

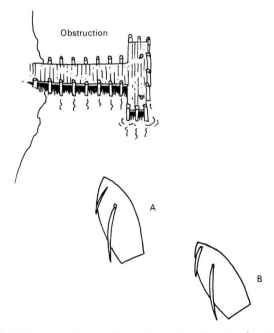

Figure 39. If A must tack to avoid an obstruction, then she must hail B asking for room to tack. B must either tack or keep clear of A

hailing yacht shall tack at once and it is the duty of the hailed yacht to keep clear. See Figure 39.

There are limitations to this rule when the obstruction is also a mark. If the hailed yacht can fetch an obstruction which is also a mark, then the hailing yacht is not entitled to room to tack, and the other yacht must hail back to say so. However, if it turns out that the hailed yacht does not fetch the mark after all, then she must retire or accept any other penalty that the race instructions may specify.

Returning to start   After the starting signal is made, a boat which has started too early returning to start again has to keep clear of all yachts which are starting correctly or have already started, until she is completely on the right side of the starting line. Thereafter, she has the same rights as any other yacht which is starting correctly, but when she gains right of way over another yacht starting correctly, she must give it ample room and opportunity to keep clear.

Re-rounding after touching a mark   If a yacht touches a mark (provided she does not consider it was the fault of another yacht), she can make amends by completing one entire rounding of the mark, leaving it on the required side, and thereafter re-rounding or re-passing it without touching it as required in the sailing instructions. See Figure 40. While exonerating herself in this way, she must keep clear of all other yachts until she has cleared the mark and is on the proper course for the next mark.

Anchored, aground or capsized   A yacht under way shall keep clear of another yacht racing which is anchored, aground or capsized, but a yacht shall not be penalised for fouling a yacht which goes aground or capsizes immediately ahead of her.

Sailing the course   A yacht shall sail the course so as to round or pass each mark on the required side in correct sequence, and so that a string representing her wake from the time she starts until she finishes would, when drawn

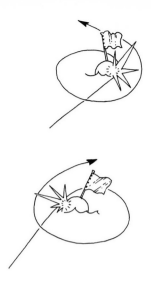

Figure 40. Correct re-rounding after hitting a port hand mark (*a*) and a starboard hand mark (*b*)

taut, lie on the required side of each mark.

Protests   If a yacht breaks one of the rules, she should retire immediately, or accept another penalty if one is specified in the race instructions. However, there may be doubt about whether a rule was broken or not, or two helmsmen may disagree about who was in the wrong. The protest is a way of resolving such disputes. If you feel that you have been fouled by another yacht, hail with the word 'Protest'. Strictly, you should also fly a protest flag as well, but in dinghy racing this is often not done. If the other helmsman agrees that he was in the wrong, he will retire and that is the end of the matter. Otherwise, you must inform the sailing committee as soon as possible, and they will arrange to hear the protest and decide what should be done. If you are involved in a protest, make a careful note of all the circumstances and any witnesses.

There is a tendency among yachtsmen to look on the protest as in some way unfriendly. If protests were made frivolously this might be so, but most race committees require a protester to pay a deposit which is only refunded if his protest is successful. A protest is a valuable way of resolving the rights and wrongs of a racing situation, and it is the only way in which an unfair competitor who breaks the rules can be punished, should he fail to acknowledge his fault. The race committee can also protest against a competitor if they see a breach of the rules.

RACING TACTICS

Sailing tactics is a wide and all-embracing subject, but it is possible to make a division into the tactics you would need to use if you were racing alone, and those you would need to try and beat other competitors. The first set of tactics is really an extension of the skills needed to make a boat go fast, as they operate to the same purpose but over a longer period of time. For example, in Figure 41 the helmsman is faced with a beat to the mark, though one tack points up better than the other. The distance sailed is the same, so which leg should he start on? In fact,

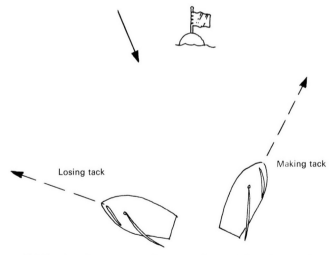

Figure 41. When beating up to a mark not exactly to windward, start off on the making tack

unless there is some other factor like the tide to consider, the best tack to start on is the making tack. There is always the possibility of a windshift before you get to the mark, so you want to make the best of what you have straight away. Also, it is easier to judge the exact moment to tack if you are close to the mark. If you do find yourself headed off by a windshift, tack as soon as you are sure it is more than a momentary fluke.

Local knowledge can play a great part in deciding this type of tactics; knowing how the wind varies round a bay or the curve of a river, where the back eddies of current run and so on, can give the local expert an edge which the visitor can hardly hope to match. Each club has its own king pin, who understands the waters round the club better than anyone else; it is a good idea to stick as closely to him as you can (if he will let you) and try to gain some of his knowledge at second hand.

Making the best use of the tide or current is an art learned afloat, because in dinghy terms, the tidal situation is very rarely as simple as most textbooks imagine. Dinghies generally sail close inshore, where minor variations of the sea bed can cause all sorts of strange effects. Perhaps the only major sin concerned with the tides is to overstand on a leg with a fair tide (Figure 42), because this means that you will have to struggle back to round the mark while people behind you who have judged things better slip happily round in front of you.

The tactics of sailing against other boats can be summed up very simply; if you are in front, defend your position. If you are behind, attack. Basically, you defend your position by keeping your boat between your opponent and the next mark. If you see him tack (on a windward leg), you should tack as well, lest he find some other wind that you have missed and slip past. If you are leading the fleet on a beat (one day!), the same principle applies. You would probably work slightly to windward of the pack, but keep a close eye on them and tack if necessary to cover the leaders.

Attacking is, as you would expect, the opposite of

defending. If you are behind on a beat, split tacks. This will force the boat ahead to tack to cover, and so you can

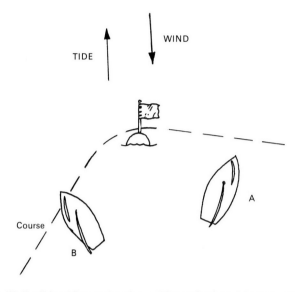

Figure 42. B will be able to tack and round the mark where A has over-stood and will have to reach or run back to the mark against a foul tide

tack again. The result is (or can be) a close tacking match in which one boat or the other will sooner or later make a mistake. The attacking boat gambles that it will not be him. One useful dodge, but which requires great skill in the execution, is the dummy tack, in which you pretend to tack, but stop on the very brink after your opponent has committed himself. The tacking duel can be great fun, and is the only way that two evenly matched boats can struggle, but there is the danger of letting other boats get by, for tacking does lose you speed. If one boat is faster than the other, then he can try attacking by bearing away, to gain extra speed, and then luffing back up to attack from leeward. Attacking from the weather side is almost certain to lead to a luffing match. An attacker can win a luffing match, but it does not happen very often.

With the wind free, attacking means using the wind shadow, which extends over about three lengths to leeward of you, to take your opponent's wind (Figure 43). On the reach, the defence is to luff the other yacht into the middle of next week. When running, the defending yacht should clear his wind, gybing if necessary, but bearing in mind the right of way rules as he does so. Another way of attacking on the run is to make use of the fact that most boats sail faster with the wind on the quarter rather than right astern. Sailing a leeward leg in two parts, gybing between each, may bring you to the leeward mark ahead of the man you want to attack.

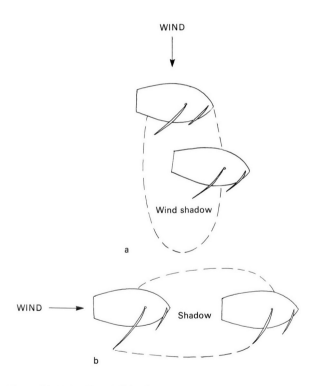

Figure 43. Using the wind shadow
a on the reach
b on the run

Racing tactics is a fascinating subject, and a much more complex one than these short notes might indicate. There are hundreds of factors to juggle with – wind, weather, sea, the psychology of your opponents and, of course, pure luck. Many people find that it is the intense mental challenge of sailboat racing which attracts them to the sport. Luck plays a large part, and your grandest and best thought-out plans can be destroyed by a flukish and unforecast windshift. But every once in a while, your planning and guessing will work out right, and you will reach the ecstatic moment when you realise that you have won!

7 Some Sailing Dinghies

Choosing a dinghy can be a difficult task, because there are about a hundred different designs, ranging from flat-out racing machines to traditionally built cruising boats. In many cases, especially if you want to race, your choice of boat has to be made in conjunction with your choice of club. While some clubs organise handicap races for mixed fleets, it is generally better to choose a boat which is sailed in some numbers by the club you choose to join.

The following list gives the basic details of some of the more popular sailing dinghies. If you want more information about any particular boat, then the best person to ask is the Secretary of the Class Association. You can get his address from the Royal Yachting Association. When writing to the RYA, it helps to enclose a stamped addressed envelope for your reply.

Although boat manufacturers are changing by degrees to metric measurements, at this time it is probably less confusing to give dimensions and weights in Imperial. Again, for information about metrication, you could get in touch with the relevant Class Association.

Name	Length ft in	Beam ft in	Weight lbs	Sail Area square ft	Remarks
Albacore	15 0	5 1	240	125	Family cruising or racing
Bonito	14 6	4 0	116	88	Single hander. Some racing
British Moth	11 0	3 11	100	63	Small single hander

	Length		Beam		Weight	Sail area	Description
Bumble Bee	8	5	4	0	65	32	Kit-built children's boat
Cadet (International Class)	10	7	4	2	120	$55\frac{1}{2}$ + spinnaker	Racing trainer for under 18s
Cherub	12	0	5	0	110	115 + spi	Exciting boat for light crews. Trapeze
Condor	16	4	7	4	210	183	Fast catamaran. Trapeze
Contender (International Class)	16	0	4	8	230	118	Single hander for experts. Trapeze
Drascombe Lugger	18	6	6	7	800	120	Day boat for coastal cruising. Smaller boats from the same stable are available
Embassy	11	0	4	8	140	72 + spi	Family boat, available as kit
Enterprise (International Class)	13	3	5	3	200	113	Very popular, widely raced
Express	12	9	5	3	154	107	Family cruiser/racer in GRP for home completion
Finn (International Class)	14	9	4	10	320	115	Olympic single hander for strong helmsmen
Fireball (International Class)	16	2	4	6	175	123 + spi	Popular two-man racing machine. Trapeze
Firefly (National Class)	12	0	4	8			Well established two-man racer
505 (International Class)	16	6	6	2	280	155 + spi	Very exciting expert's boat. Trapeze
Fleetwind	12	2	4	6	140	95	Club racing
Flying Dutchman (International Class)	19	11	5	7	364	200 + spi	Olympic two-man racing. For experts. Trapeze
Flying Fifteen (National Class)	20	0	5	0	675	150 + spi	Popular racing keelboat
420 (International Class)	13	9	5	5	220	110 + spi	Training boat for Olympic 470, or racing on its own
470 (International Class)	15	5	5	6	260	143 + spi	Olympic two-man boat
GP14	14	0	5	0	285	102	Popular racer/cruiser. Often built at home
Graduate (National Class)	12	6	4	9	185	90	Family cruiser/racer
Gull	11	0	5	3	160	70 + spi	Well established racing dinghy
Heron	11	3	4	6	140	70	Gunter rigged general purpose boat

Boat	Length		Beam		Weight	Price	Description
Hornet	16	0	4	7		140 + spi	High speed two-man racing. Trapeze
Ideal	12	3	5	3	182	95	Kit-built general purpose family boat
International 14 (International Class)	14	0	5	6	225	160 + spi	Specialised boat for experts
Lark	13	4	5	6	200	105 + spi	Club racing
Laser (International Class)	13	11	4	6	150	76	Very popular single hander. Fast growing class
Minisail	13	0	3	8	112	80	Single-handed racer
Miracle	12	9	5	3	169	95	Plywood racer/cruiser built from a kit
Mirror	10	10	4	7	135	69 + spi	Hugely popular family cruiser/racer built from a kit
National 18 (National Class)	18	0	6	0	550	190 + spi	Well established cruiser/racer
National 12 (National Class)	12	0	6	0	200	90	Popular development class. Many different designs
OK (International Class)	13	2	4	8	159	92	Una rigged single hander
Optimist (International Class)	7	7	3	9	77	35	Originally a basic trainer, now offers international racing for children as well
Osprey (National Class)	17	6	5	9	295	150 + spi	A powerful boat for two or three-man crews
Scorpion (National Class)	14	0	4	10	180	107 + spi	High speed two-man racer
Shearwater (National Class)	16	6	7	5	255	163 + spi	Well established catamaran. Trapeze
Signet	12	5	4	9	155	88 + spi	Cruiser/racer
Snipe (International Class)	15	6	5	0	381	115	International racer. Now quite old
Solo	12	5	5	3	155	90	Una rigged single hander
Streaker	12	9	4	7	100	70	Light boat for one or two, which can be built from a kit
Topper	11	0	3	10	110	56	Una rigged single hander
Tornado (International Class)	20	0	10	0	276	235	Olympic catamaran
Wayfarer	15	10	6	1	365	125 + spi	Training or long-distance cruising. Also racer
Wineglass	15	0	5	10	230	123	Racing or cruising

8   Useful Information

ASSOCIATIONS

Royal Yachting Association
Victoria Way
Woking
Surrey GU21 1EQ

BOOK LIST

This is Sailing, by Richard Creagh-Osborne (Nautical Publishing Company Ltd).
This is Racing, by Richard Creagh-Osborne (Nautical Publishing Company Ltd).
First Steps in Small Boat Sailing, by P G Hansen and Bent Aarre (Adlard Coles Ltd). (Mostly about the Optimist dinghy)
Build and Sail Your Own Boat, by Norman Dahl (Stanley Paul Ltd). (Mostly about the Ideal dinghy)
International Yacht Racing Rules (Royal Yachting Association, Victoria Way, Woking, Surrey GU21 1EQ).
Sail Racer by Jack Knight (Adlard Coles Ltd).
Sailing Strategy, by Ian Proctor (Adlard Coles Ltd).
Dinghies for All Waters by Eric Coleman (Hollis and Carter Ltd).
The Dinghy Owner's Handbook by Dave Jenkins (Hollis and Carter Ltd).

Glossary

ABACK A sail is set aback when it is sheeted on the opposite side to normal (to weather)

ABEAM Away to one side of the boat, at right angles to the fore-and-aft line

ASLEEP A sail is asleep when it is full and drawing

BEARING AWAY Altering course away from the direction of the wind

BEATING Working the boat against the wind in a zig-zag series of tacks

BOOM The spar along the foot of a sail

BOW The front part of the boat

BY THE LEE When running and the wind comes over the same side of the boat as the boom is being carried – a dangerous condition

CENTREBOARD A lifting keel used to prevent the boat slipping sideways

CLEAT A fitting to which a rope can be made fast

CLEW The unsupported corner of a sail, to which the sheet is attached

CLOSE-HAULED Sailing as close to the wind as is possible

DOWNHAUL A line used to pull something down, in particular the spinnaker pole

EASING SHEETS Letting out the sheets to adjust the set of the sails

FOOT The bottom edge of the sail

GAFF The spar which carries the head of the mainsail in gunter rig

GOING ABOUT Tacking; going from one tack to the other

GUY A line used to control the fore-and-aft position of the spinnaker pole

GYBING Turning the stern of the boat through the eye of the wind so that the boat goes from one tack to the other

HALYARD A line to haul a sail up the mast

HARDENING SHEETS Pulling the sheets in to adjust the sail

HEAD The top corner of a sail, to which the halyard is generally attached

HEAD TO WIND With the bow pointing into wind

JIB The sail a dinghy carries forward of the mast

KICKING STRAP A line or purchase used to hold the boom down, preventing it from lifting

LEECH The rear edge of a sail

LEEWARD (pronounced loo-ard). On the side of an object away from the direction of the wind

LEEWAY The unwanted motion of a boat sideways and downwind

LUFF The front edge of a sail

LUFFING Altering course towards the direction of the wind

MAINSAIL The sail a dinghy carries behind the mast

OUTHAUL A line used to haul something out, in particular the clew of the mainsail out along the boom

PAINTER A line attached to the bow, used to secure the boat to the shore

PINCHING Sailing too close to the wind, so that the boat slows down

PLANING When a suitable hull travels at high speed over the top of the water, rather than pushing the water aside

PORT The left-hand side of the boat

QUARTER The side of a boat between the beam and the stern

REACHING The point of sailing between close-hauled and running

REEFING Reducing the area of a sail, generally because of strong winds

RUNNING When the wind is coming over the stern

RUNNING RIGGING Lines which are adjusted as the boat sails along, such as sheets, halyards etc

SHEET The line attached to the clew of a sail to control it

SPAR A pole used to support an edge of a sail (but not including the mast)

SPINNAKER A large, light sail set when running and reaching

SPINNAKER POLE A spar used to hold out the tack of the spinnaker

SPRIT A spar which supports a sail by going diagonally across it

STANDING RIGGING Rigging which is not normally adjusted when under way, such as the shrouds and forestay which support the mast

STARBOARD The right-hand side of the boat

STEM The very front of a boat with a sharp bow

STERN The back of the boat

TACK The lower forward corner of a sail

TACKING Changing from one tack to the other by turning through the wind

TIDAL STREAM Horizontal movement of the water caused by the rise and fall of the tide

TIDE Vertical rise and fall of water in seas and oceans, caused by the attraction of the sun and moon

TILLER The lever connected to the rudder, with which the boat is steered

TOESTRAPS Straps for the feet to support the crew when sitting out to keep their boat level

TRAPEZE A harness used to support a crewman outside the boat

UPHAUL A line used to haul something up, in particular the spinnaker pole (also known as a topping lift)

WARP A strong line used for anchoring or towing

WEATHER SIDE The side of an object upon which the wind blows